LIGHT ★ THE ★ CANDLES! BEAT ★ THE ★ DRUMS!

A Book of Holidays

By Jane Sarnoff and Reynold Ruffins

To Joanna - - - so she will always know when

Charles Scribner's Sons, New York

JANUARY

1 New Year's Day All over the world the New Year is greeted with noise. Bam! Crash! Bells, horns, gongs, guns, rockets, and firecrackers blare and blast to frighten off the evil spirits which — it was said — gathered to bring bad luck to the New Year. Masks, first worn to confuse evil spirits by hiding joyful faces, are still part of New Year parties. The New Year has often been thought the right time to get your life back in order. Debts should be paid or forgiven. People should make resolutions to lead a better life in the year to come. Gifts are sometimes given on New Year's Eve, but there is a wide-spread superstition against giving gifts on New Year's Day. It was thought that good luck would be given away with the gift. Another New Year superstition to take note of: Don't hang a new calendar before New Year's Day or some of the old year's bad luck will enter the New Year.

Long before there were calendars, before time was divided into months and years, there was rejoicing at important annual events (see October 31). People celebrated the first blooms after the time of cold, the first rains after the dry period, the time when sheep or camels gave birth. Many nations now celebrate the beginning of the year on the first of January, but this is a "modern" custom. In the late 1500s, Italian astronomers developed a new solar calendar of 365 days to replace an ancient Roman calendar which had a year of 355 days (see April 1). When the calendar was changed, the start of the year was put on the first of January, about the time the earth is closest to the sun. Before the change most of Europe celebrated the New Year at the time of the Vernal Equinox (see March 21) or the first full moon in spring, usually at the end of March. England and its colonies — including what is now the United States — did not use the new calendar or the "new" New Year date until the mid-1700s.

January 1, 2000 will not be the first day of the twenty-first century. The modern system of dating begins with January 1 of the year 1 — not the year 0 — so that the new century will begin on January 1, 2001.

Throughout this book, **Admission Day** refers to the anniversary of admission to the United States of America as a state; **Ratification Day** refers to the anniversary of ratification of the Constitution of the United States of America by the original thirteen states.

2 Isaac Asimov's Birthday
3 Alaska—Admission Day
4 Utah—Admission Day
5 Twelfth Night of Christmas

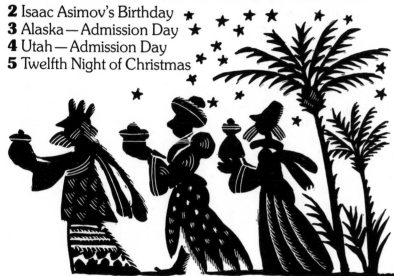

6 Epiphany, Twelfth Day, Three Kings' Day Long before the birth of Jesus, the Egyptians had a holiday on the day we call the sixth of January. On that day the Egyptians honored the Nile River, believing that the water was at its purest and ready for use in holy ceremonies. When Christianity reached Egypt, it was natural for the new Egyptian Christians to think that Jesus must have been baptized on the day on which the water was most pure. And so the Eastern church celebrated Epiphany—the commemoration of the baptism of Jesus—on the sixth of January. When, hundreds of years later, the date for the celebration of the birth of Jesus was set on the twenty-fifth of December, the sixth of January was also celebrated as the Twelfth Day of Christmas. In many countries the

sixth of January is thought to be the day on which the three Magi, or kings, brought gifts to the infant Jesus. In some places gifts are given on this day as well as, or instead of, on Christmas. Children dress in the costumes of the kings, and there are processions in the streets and parties at home.

8 Battle of New Orleans—Louisiana
9 Connecticut—Ratification Day

15 Martin Luther King, Jr.'s, Birthday Martin Luther King, Jr., was a black civil rights leader and clergyman in the southern United States in the 1950s and 1960s. At that time, throughout much of the South, black people had separate and often less good schools, housing, and places for recreation and entertainment. Blacks had to ride in the back of public buses and streetcars, they could not eat in "white only" restaurants or drink from "white only" water fountains. Often black people were stopped from registering to vote in elections and so they had little chance of electing officials who wanted to change the laws. Dr. King led the fight against these injustices, against the written and unwritten laws of segregation in the South and the North. His way of fighting was nonviolent. He organized sit-ins and led large numbers of blacks and concerned whites to peacefully boycott—stay away from—stores, bus lines, and other businesses that treated blacks unfairly. Often he and those he led were arrested and jailed. Slowly, however, his work helped to change laws and social practices. In 1964, Dr. King was awarded the Nobel peace prize for his leadership in the civil rights movement. On April 4, 1968, Dr. King's beliefs and actions led to his death by an assassin's bullet. His birth date, or a time close to it, is now celebrated in many communities in the United States where his ideas and achievements are honored.

16 National Nothing Day So many days of the year are officially designated as a time to celebrate, honor, or observe something that this day has been unofficially set aside as a day on which to celebrate, honor, or observe absolutely nothing. Unless, of course, it's your birthday.

There are no official United States of America Holidays!

There are really no national holidays in the United States.

Each state decides on its own holidays by legislative

enactment or proclamation by the state executive. Most

states, however, follow the federal legal public holidays,

even though, by law, the president and Congress can only

proclaim holidays for Washington, D.C., and federal employees.

See page 32.

17 Benjamin Franklin's Birthday Benjamin Franklin was an American Revolutionary leader, a statesman and diplomat, an inventor, a writer, and a printer. He was born in Boston in 1706 and apprenticed to his brother, a printer, when he was twelve. When he was seventeen, he ran away to Philadelphia. He worked there as a printer, opened his own print shop, and later published *The Gazette.* His writings included *Poor Richard's Almanac,* which is still read for its wise sayings: "Early to bed and early to rise, makes a man healthy, wealthy, and wise." Or "A penny saved is a penny earned."

Franklin was postmaster of Philadelphia...until he was fired. But while he lived in the city he started the first public library in the world and set up a fire department. He also planned the paving and lighting of the streets, the first city hospital in the colonies, and the school that became the University of Pennsylvania. He invented many things — the lightning rod, bifocal glasses, a glass harmonica, a metal heating stove, and methods of soil fertilization — but he did not patent them because he believed that his inventions should be free to all. His scientific discoveries included the identification of electricity in lightning.

Franklin helped to write and was one of the signers of the Declaration of Independence (see July 4). He was also a member of the convention that wrote the Constitution of the United States. Franklin tried to outlaw slavery in the Constitution, and when he failed at that, became the president of the first antislavery society in the United States. His birthday was first celebrated in 1826 by a group of Boston printers.

What did Benjamin Franklin say when he discovered electricity?
Nothing, he was too shocked.

23 John Hancock's Birthday John Hancock was one of the leaders of the American Revolution. He is best known, however, as the first signer of the Declaration of Independence (see July 4). And he signed his name big, he explained, so that the King of England could read the name "without spectacles." Because of this, his birthday is also celebrated as National Handwriting Day.

26 Michigan — Admission Day

27 Wolfgang Amadeus Mozart's Birthday Mozart was a European composer of music in the eighteenth century. His father was also a musician and taught him, so that by the time Mozart was six he could play the harpsichord, violin, and organ well enough to perform for royalty. He began to compose music when he was five. Although Mozart died when he was a young man, he left us some very beautiful music in many forms — from operas to funny songs and cheerful dances.

*The Romans thought that even numbers were unlucky,
so all their months had 29 or 31 days except February.
February could have 28 days, since it was already an unlucky month,
a time when people were supposed to make sacrifices
to cleanse themselves of past sins.*

2 Groundhog Day In ancient Rome the second day of February was a day of worship of the mother of the great god Mars. Candles and torches were carried through the streets to the temples in her honor. When Christianity became an important religion in Rome, the ceremony turned into one of honor for Mary, the mother of Jesus. The candles were carried into the church where a mass was held, and the day became known as Candlemas Day. Because Candlemas Day comes in midwinter, when people start to think about spring, the date was often used to predict the weather for the rest of the season. Throughout much of Europe, it was said that "If Candlemas Day is fair and clear, there'll be two winters in the year." In other parts of Europe — Germany, Austria, and the far North — weather predictions were based on the weather on the day hibernating animals came out of their nests, usually in early February.

Early American colonists followed traditional Candlemas Day beliefs. Later, German settlers in Pennsylvania kept the date of Candlemas, but added the custom of using hibernating animals to foretell the weather. And the groundhog, or woodchuck, was the most common hibernating animal in Pennsylvania. According to superstition, if the groundhog comes out of its underground nest on February 2 and sees its shadow, there will be six more weeks of winter. If the day is cloudy and there is no shadow, the groundhog will stay out of its nest, spring will soon arrive, and farmers can safely plant their spring crops. (See February 14.)

Throughout this book holidays that have no regular dates according to the Western civil calendar are placed where they most often fall during the year. Lunar holidays are marked with a ◗ ; movable civil holidays are marked with a ★ .

◗ **Lunar New Year** Before European astronomers discovered that it took earth 365 days to circle the sun and developed a year long solar calendar based on that time period, Asian astronomers had developed an accurate yearly lunar calendar. The lunar calendar is based on the waxing and waning of the moon; each full cycle is a month. There are twelve lunar months in each year, with a "leap" month inserted from time to time to keep the lunar year in cycle with the seasons.

The beginning of the lunar year comes at different times in different countries. The Moslem lunar calendar does not have a leap month, so that the time of the new year in relation to the Western calendar changes each year. The Jewish New Year always falls in the autumn of the Western calendar. And the calendar used by China and other Asian countries begins the lunar year at sunset or moonrise of the day following the second new moon after the Winter Solstice (see December 22). On the calendar used in the United States—the Western, or civil, calendar — the Chinese lunar new year always falls between January 21 and February 19. The holiday is celebrated very much like the solar new year with the addition of community parades—often with dragon floats and firecrackers—and extended family parties.

Chinese lunar years are grouped into units of twelve, and these years have names—just like our months. Anyone whose birthday is in January or the first few weeks of February was born in the lunar year before the one given for his or her birth year.

Rat	Ox	Tiger	Rabbit	Dragon	Snake
1936	1937	1938	1939	1940	1941
1948	1949	1950	1951	1952	1953
1960	1961	1962	1963	1964	1965
1972	1973	1974	1975	1976	1977
Horse	**Ram**	**Monkey**	**Rooster**	**Dog**	**Pig**
1942	1943	1944	1945	1946	1947
1954	1955	1956	1957	1958	1959
1966	1967	1968	1969	1970	1971
1978	1979	1980	1981	1982	1983

6 Massachusetts—Ratification Day

12 Abraham Lincoln's Birthday Abraham Lincoln was the sixteenth president of the United States. His birthday was first celebrated publicly in 1866, the year after his death by an assassin's bullet. Lincoln's birthday, or a day close to it, is now a legal holiday in many places, but is still not celebrated in over half the states. During Lincoln's term in office, the Civil War started and ended. An ugly, bitter struggle over slavery between friends and families, the war was still in full force when Lincoln went to Gettysburg, Pennsylvania, to dedicate a soldiers' cemetery. There he gave one of the noblest public speeches ever given. Lincoln's Gettysburg Address was not — as popular stories go — written at the last moment on the back of an envelope. It was carefully and deeply considered and still has important meaning for the United States.

Lincoln's Gettysburg Address

"Four score and seven years ago, our fathers brought forth on this continent a new nation conceived in liberty and dedicated to the proposition that all men are created equal. Now we are engaged in a great civil war testing whether that nation, or any nation so conceived and so dedicated, can long endure. We are met on a great battlefield of that war. We have come to dedicate a portion of that field as a final resting-place for those who here gave their lives that that nation might live. It is altogether fitting and proper that we should do this. But, in a larger sense, we cannot dedicate, we cannot consecrate, we cannot hallow this ground. The brave men, living and dead, who struggled here have consecrated it far above our poor power to add or detract. The world will little note nor long remember what we say here, but it can never forget what they did here. It is for us the living rather to be dedicated here to the unfinished work which they who fought here have thus far so nobly advanced. It is rather for us to be here dedicated to the great task remaining before us—that from these honored dead we take increased devotion to that cause for which they gave the last full measure of devotion—that we here highly resolve that these dead shall not have died in vain, that this nation under God shall have a new birth of freedom, and that government of the people, by the people, for the people, shall not perish from the earth."

14 St. Valentine's Day In ancient Rome — where many of our holidays began — the fifteenth of February was thought to be the day on which birds and other small animals chose their mates. On that day each unmarried Roman girl put her name on a slip of paper and put the paper into a large jar. Each unmarried Roman boy took a slip from the jar and read the name of his sweetheart. When the Roman army invaded England, the soldiers took the custom of choosing sweethearts with them. There had been an earlier practice in England of wearing a lover's "favor" — a small handkerchief or other piece of material — pinned to a sleeve. So the English boys added to the Roman custom by drawing hearts around the name they chose from the jar and pinning the paper to a sleeve. From this practice came the saying "To wear your heart on your sleeve," meaning to show your love to the whole world.

At least two St. Valentines may have given the present holiday its name. Both were put to death on February 14 during the third century A.D. by the Roman emperor. The first Valentine was killed because he continued to perform marriages after the emperor had forbidden them. (The emperor had been having trouble getting married and engaged men to go off to war!) The other Valentine had been jailed for helping Christians. He fell in love with his jailer's daughter, cured her blindness, and wrote her love notes. He signed the notes just as we do today, "From your Valentine." At first the Christian holiday was religious, a memorial for the Valentines. Gradually, however, the new holiday and the old became one, celebrating love and lovers on February 14 and called St. Valentine's Day.

In some parts of the southern United States, February 14 is also Groundhog Day (see February 2). The combination seems logical: On St. Valentine's Day small animals were originally thought to come out of their nests to mate; on Groundhog Day, small animals are thought to come out of their nests to help predict the weather.

15 Susan B. Anthony's Birthday Susan B. Anthony fought for women's rights in the United States. In 1837 she led the struggle for coeducation and college training for girls. She helped to get laws passed so that a woman's property — or her children — could not be taken away from her by her husband, father, or male guardian. And Susan B. Anthony fought, as women are still fighting, for equal pay. In 1872 she was arrested, tried, and fined for leading a group of women to the polls to vote. Women in the United States did not get the right to vote until 1920. (See August 26.)

22 George Washington's Birthday George Washington was the first president of the United States. His birthday was first celebrated by the nation in 1796, the year before he died. But the date when his birthday is, or was, celebrated is a little confusing. He was born on February 11, 1732, according to the Old Style calendar then in use. When the calendar changed twenty years later (see January 1), Washington's birthday changed to February 22. But, that's just his birthday — that's not when we celebrate it. George Washington's birthday is legally observed in all states and Puerto Rico on the third Monday in February — no matter what the date. In some places, the holiday is not even called Washington's Birthday. In Hawaii it is called President's Day, in Arizona Washington's Day, in Minnesota Founder's Day; and in Ohio, South Dakota, Wisconsin, and Wyoming it is called Washington/Lincoln Day.

29 Leap Day Leap year does *not* occur every four years. An extra day is added only to years that can be divided by four. Century years — 1800, 1900, 2000 — are leap years only when they can be divided by 400.

Washington and Lincoln were alike because they were both presidents. How were they different? Lincoln once lived in Washington, but Washington never lived in Lincoln.

MARCH

3 National Anthem Day On this day in 1931 the "Star Spangled Banner" was adopted as the national anthem of the United States. The words were written by Francis Scott Key during a naval battle in Baltimore harbor in the War of 1812 (see June 14). The tune is an old English drinking song.

5 Boston Massacre Day—Massachusetts

☽**Purim** Four hundred years before the birth of Jesus—by Jewish dating 400 B.C.E., or Before the Common Era—the Jews fell under the rule of the king of Persia. Haman, a wicked advisor to the king, wanted to kill all the Jews. To decide on which day the killings would take place, he cast lots. The word *purim* probably comes from a Persian word meaning "lot" or "chance." Haman's plot did not succeed because of the efforts of the Jew Mordecai and his cousin Esther. Purim is celebrated on the fourteenth of the Hebrew month of Adar with costume parties, songs and stories of the narrow escape, and special cakes and candies.

The Hebrew year is based on a lunar calendar (see February: Lunar New Year). It has twelve months with the periodic addition of a "leap" month. The Jewish holidays are always on the same day in the Hebrew calendar, but they fall on different dates in the civil, or Western, calendar. In a Hebrew leap year there are two months of Adar. When this happens, Purim is celebrated on the fourteenth day of Adar II. Although Purim is usually in February, in leap years it is in March. Passover is usually in March, but can be in April—and almost always is during leap years.

September		March	
	Tishri		Nisan
October		April	
	Heshvan		Iyar
November		May	
	Kislev		Sivan
December		June	
	Teveth		Tammuz
January		July	
	Shevat		Ab
February		August	
	Adar		Elul

☽**Passover** Passover, one of the most important Jewish holidays, is celebrated for eight days. It starts on the eve of the fifteenth of the Hebrew month of Nisan. In 1300 B.C.E. the Jews had been slaves in Egypt for 210 years. Passover is the holiday of independence which marks the Jews' exodus, or leaving, of Egypt under the leadership of Moses. The holiday is celebrated with seders, special dinners at which the history of the exodus is told. The last supper eaten by Jesus and his apostles may have been a seder.

★**National Procrastination Week** National Procrastination Week is celebrated sometime in March…whenever procrastinators get around to it, but usually a week or two late. The procrastinators don't complain about the lateness of their holiday; they believe that procrastination shows faith in the future. (See September 5.)

17 St. Patrick's Day St. Patrick, the patron saint of Ireland, is honored by the Irish and all their friends with parades and parties. The wearing of a green article of clothing on March 17 shows a wish to take part in the St. Patrick's Day fun.

21 The Vernal Equinox The date on which the sun crosses the celestial equator from south to north is called the Vernal Equinox. The crossing marks the beginning of spring in the Northern Hemisphere. On that date, usually March 21, day and night are of equal length, after which the days start to get longer. (See September 23.)

24 Harry Houdini's Birthday Harry Houdini was once handcuffed and put in a trunk that was sealed, chained, and thrown underwater. A few minutes later he took his bows from the shore. Houdini, an American magician and writer (1874–1926), was known throughout the world as an escape artist. He could get out of straitjackets, handcuffs, chains, and locks of every type. He even escaped from locked jail cells.

25 Maryland Day

31 Seward's Day—Alaska Alaska was purchased from Russia by the United States in 1867 for two cents an acre.

The Hebrew word for calendar is luach.

When Houdini was wrapped in chains inside a sealed jail cell, what kind of party did he want most? A coming-out party.

Why did Harry Houdini fear the letter E before he tried a death-defying escape? Because E is at the end of life.

A hundred people can't stand me on my end, but one person can carry me. What am I? A rope.

APRIL

1 April Fool's Day On April Fool's Day we play tricks on people and may even send them on foolish or impossible errands. But how did this tradition begin? The ancient Romans told the story of the young Proserpina. As she played in the meadow, her lap full of wild flowers, Pluto, the king of the Underworld, swooped her up and carried her away to be queen of his kingdom. Proserpina's mother, Ceres, arrived just in time to hear the echoes of her daughter's screams and to see the flowers blown in every direction by the late March winds. Ceres' search for her daughter — following the echoes and chasing the flowers — was considered a fool's errand. The Romans remembered Ceres' plight by sending each other on silly errands on the last days of March. This may have been the way April Fool's Day began.

Or April Fool's Day may have begun in France in 1582. That year the pope announced the introduction of a new calendar (see January 1). The New Year was to begin on the first of January; it could no longer be celebrated at the time of the Vernal Equinox (see March 21) or, as was often the custom, a few days later on April 1. When the first "old" New Year's Day came around, some people still had not understood or heard about the change in the calendar. The confusion provided a perfect opportunity for playing tricks. And the new opportunity to trick tied in with an old French saying. In France, young fish appear in the rivers early in April—fish that are far easier to catch than the older ones. A silly or easily tricked person was called *poisson d'avril,* which means "April fish." And that is what April fools are called in France today. But French children don't seem to mind — perhaps because it is the custom to give children a chocolate fish on April 1.

The day of trickery and fools' errands spread from France to the British Isles. In England on April 1, people were sent to get a pint of pigeon's milk, or to buy a left-handed hammer. In Scotland those who fell for the tricks were called "gowks," because they were often sent hunting for the nonexistent

Why are you so tired on April Fool's Day?
Because you have just had a March of 31 days.

gowk. In India similar tricks have been played for thousands of years at the Huli Festival on March 31, but the similarity of dates and customs is probably a coincidence.

European settlers brought the April Fool's custom to the American colonies. Today people still call the zoo asking for Mr. Fox, tell younger brothers and sisters that they have a terrible case of "earlobes," or send the unsuspecting to the library for a biography of Eve's mother.

2 Hans Christian Andersen's Birthday

3 Washington Irving's Birthday

5 Booker T. Washington's Birthday

◗ **Easter** A spring festival celebrating the return of the warm sun to the earth is one of the earliest known holidays. It has been celebrated in every part of the world where there is a cold season. The name *Easter,* however, most likely came from the northern parts of Europe. There, many years before Christianity, people worshiped a spring goddess, Osters, or in the language of the British Isles, Eostre. Eostre, who was often also a goddess of the dawn or the east — the direction from which the sun rises — was honored each year with a spring festival. As a symbol of the renewed life of the sun, eggs were sometimes colored, decorated, and exchanged as gifts. Some were buried in the fields as the first crops began to rise from the soil. As Christianity moved across Europe, people wove the old religions and the new together. Christian meanings were given to the old customs. The holiday of Eostre, marking the rebirth of the sun, became the celebration of the resurrection of Jesus. Eggs continued to be decorated as part of the Christian holiday. Rabbits or hares were often the first animals born in the spring in England, and one of the old gods was thought to take the form of a rabbit during the full spring moon. So the rabbit, too, became part of the Christian celebration of Easter.

Long before the celebrations for either Eostre or Jesus, however, there was probably an "Easter" parade in the spring.

Just as the earth puts on new clothes—all green and flowered — in the spring, people have also worn new clothes and flowers in their hair or hats since ancient times. Often, people would join together, dancing or marching around, wearing their new clothes in joy and with hopes of good luck in the year to come. It is still considered good luck to wear new clothes at Easter time.

The sun dances when it rises on Easter morning./Very old European superstition

Easter is one of the few holidays in the Christian calendar that is still celebrated according to the moon. It is observed by most Christians on the first Sunday after the full moon that falls on or just after the Vernal Equinox (see March 21). The earliest day that Easter can be is March 22, as occurred in 1818, but won't happen again in either the twentieth or twenty-first century. The latest day on which Easter can fall is April 25, but that will not happen until 2038.

13 Thomas Jefferson's Birthday The third president of the United States, Thomas Jefferson, could speak not only English, but Greek, French, Italian, Latin, and Spanish. To celebrate his birthday, learn how to say "Happy Birthday" in all five foreign languages.

18 Anniversary of Paul Revere's Ride

23 William Shakespeare's Birthday

24 Yom Hashoa Yom Hashoa, or Holocaust Day, is a memorial day for the millions of Jews killed by the Nazis during World War II.

✦**Arbor Day/Bird Day** Trees are a strange and wonderful combination of beauty and usefulness. From them we get food, shade, firewood, houses to live in, boats to go to sea on, paper to write on. And still trees are beautiful from season to season. For thousands of years people have worshiped trees, planted sacred groves and avenues, and held festivals in trees' honor. In the United States, Arbor Day is celebrated by many states in April or May — the best times for planting young trees. Bird Day is often celebrated at the same time. Perhaps birds have as much reason to praise trees as people do.

Daylight saving time begins at 2:00 A.M. on the last Sunday in April.

How can you tell a dogwood tree from a pine tree?
By its bark.

MAY

1 May Day The first known May celebrations, in Egypt and India, were spring festivals held at the time of the full flowering of plants and trees. Later, in ancient Rome, Flora—the goddess of spring—was honored with festivities lasting from April 28 to May 3. In the middle of this celebration another holiday honored the goddess Maia on the first of the month named after her. Flowers and fruits were given as gifts by adults, while children exchanged dolls made from flowers. Men sent family or good friends a young flowering tree to be planted with flowers and good luck-bringing herbs around its base. In medieval England May Day was sometimes celebrated by dancing around a flowering tree or more often a May pole. A tall pole was set in the ground and decorated with flowers and streamers that hung down from the top. Dancers took the loose ends of the streamers and circled the pole. A May queen and court was often chosen to rule over the merrymaking. "Wars" were fought with flowers and lovers went "a Maying" — they took walks in the fields, making baskets of flowers and wreaths of grasses for each other.

In old England it was believed that you could make freckles disappear by washing your face with dew, before dawn, while facing east on the first of May.

May Day celebrations were brought to the American Colonies by some settlers, but the day was far too worldly for the Puritans. May poles were cut down and the holiday was forbidden. In other countries, too, the holiday was thought to be too lighthearted — many felt that times were hard, holidays should be serious, people more thoughtful. May Day, in most times and places, has been celebrated in seasons of plenty, when food and gifts are free for the picking and making. It has been a holiday of the people, of the peasants rather than the rich and upper classes. Today, throughout most of the world, May Day honors the importance and solidarity of the working class. Although most of the flowers are gone, the holiday is still one for the people.

What can a woman be that a man never can?
A mother.

★**Be Kind to Animals Week** The week starting with the first Sunday in May is celebrated by many as Be Kind to Animals Week. This week is observed to bring attention to the needs of all living creatures and to remind us to take proper care of pets.

The cat is the only domestic animal not mentioned in the Bible.

A squirrel can climb up a tree trunk faster than it can run on level ground.

A chameleon's tongue and body are the same length.

A zebra is black; its stripes are white.

5 Cinco de Mayo Most of California and the southwestern United States once belonged to Mexico. Each year, on the Fifth of May — Cinco de Mayo — the Mexican background of many of the citizens and communities of the United States is celebrated. There are speeches, parades with costumed riders, music, dancing, and foods — all with a Mexican/American flavor.

10 Golden Spike Day The anniversary of the joining — with a golden spike — of the Union Pacific and Central Pacific railways in 1869.

★ **Mother's Day** The second Sunday in May is annually designated as Mother's Day by presidential proclamation (see page 32). The holiday was first celebrated in Philadelphia in 1907, when Anna Jarvis asked her church to hold a special service for all mothers in memory of her mother. The idea and the date of the holiday spread throughout the United States and then to much of the world. Miss Jarvis, who had wanted the holiday to stay within the church, grew bitter at the popularity of sending cards, flowers, and candy. Mother's Day became a federal holiday in the United States in 1914, but other countries had earlier, less widely celebrated, Mother's Days. In eastern Europe Mother's Day was held just before Christmas; and from the 1600s until the mid-1800s the English celebrated Mothering Sunday in mid-Lent, giving flowers and small cakes as gifts.

12 Florence Nightingale's Birthday

★**Armed Forces Day** By Presidential proclamation (see page 32) the third Sunday of May honors the armed forces of the United States.

★**Victoria Day/Sovereign's Birthday** In Canada the first Monday before May 25 of each year is set aside to honor Queen Victoria and to celebrate the birthday — no matter when it really is — of the present sovereign of the Commonwealth.

23 South Carolina — Ratification Day

25 African Freedom Day The Organization for African Unity was formed on May 25, 1963. On May 25 of each year the member nations celebrate their independence from colonial rule with songs, dances, sporting events, and speeches.

◐**Dragon Boat Festival** In China the fifth day of the fifth month of the lunar year (see February 5: Lunar New Year) is observed as a day of honor in memory of Ch'u Yuan, a poet-statesman of the fourth century B.C. There are boat races in dragon-shaped boats, and poems are read and special foods are eaten at family parties.

★ **Memorial Day** Throughout the ages countries have proclaimed special days on which to remember those who gave their lives for their country. In the United States the last Monday in May or May 30 is observed in most states as Memorial or Decoration Day. Graves are decorated with flowers, and there are marches and other tributes for the war dead. Memorial Days have been widely celebrated in the United States from the Civil War years. At Gettysburg National Cemetery, the cemetery opened by President Lincoln with his Gettysburg Address (see February 12), there are parades and services in which schoolchildren put flowers on graves of the unknown soldiers.

29 Rhode Island — Ratification Day
Wisconsin — Admission Day

30 St. Joan of Arc's Day

Joan of Arc was burned at the stake after being found guilty of many charges. One of the charges was that she disobeyed her parents.

When do monsters give presents to their mothers?
On Mummy's Day.

JUNE

1 Tennessee and Kentucky — Admission Day

2 Italy — National Holiday

5 World Environment Day Since 1972 the United Nations has requested that all nations mark this day with activities showing concern for the care and preservation of the environment.

6 Denmark — Constitution Day
Sweden — Flag Day

★**The Rice God Day** In Japan rice is the most important grain. In some parts of Japan the first Sunday of June is dedicated to festivities in honor of the Shinto god of rice, Sanbai-sama. The festival, which is centuries old, is celebrated with parades in traditional costumes, music, dancing, and prayers to the god.

★**Children's Sunday** The second Sunday in June is observed as Children's Sunday in many Christian churches in the United States. In Massachusetts the same day, called Children's Day, is a state holiday and many people want the day recognized nationally by presidential proclamation. (See page 32.)

11 King Kamehameha Day — Hawaii

★**National Flag Week** By annual presidential proclamation (see page 32) the week that includes June 14 is National Flag Week.

14 Flag Day In Philadelphia on the fourteenth of June in 1777, John Adams introduced the following resolution to the Continental Congress: "Resolved, that the Flag of the United States be 13 stripes alternate red and white, that the Union be 13 stars white in a blue field representing a new constellation."

When Vermont joined the Union of the original thirteen states in 1791 and Kentucky in 1792, an act of Congress increased the number of stars and stripes to fifteen. This flag was used for the next twenty-three years and inspired Francis Scott Key to write the "Star Spangled Banner" (see March 3). As more states joined the Union, it became impossible to add a new star and stripe for each state — the flag would have been gigantic! It was decided that the flag would return to thirteen stripes and that on the admission of each new state one star would be added to the blue field. The fifty-star flag has been flown since July 4, 1960, after Hawaii joined the Union.

The story about Betsy Ross making a flag for George Washington and a committee of Congress is just that — a story. Equally imaginary is the tale of the young women from Portsmouth, New Hampshire, making a Stars and Stripes flag from ball gowns for John Paul Jones to take into battle.

The flag was over a hundred years old before a special celebration was held in its honor. In 1893 the mayor of Philadelphia held the first Flag Day in the United States displaying flags from all public buildings and in all schools. Since 1950, June 14 has been officially observed as Flag Day.

Flags have long been carried into battle and kept near the king as a sign that he was unharmed. When the flag was captured or knocked to the ground, the enemy was dangerously near to the king. It therefore became "unlucky" for a flag to touch the ground even in times of peace.

★**Father's Day** Like Mother's Day (see May: Mother's Day), the modern Father's Day in the United States was started by a woman who wanted to honor her own parent. In 1910 Mrs. John Dodd of Spokane, Washington, asked her church to have a special father's service on June 5, her father's birthday. The ministers of the city decided that the special service was a good idea, but chose to hold it on the third Sunday in June, the day on which it is now celebrated by presidential proclamation (see page 32). Many other countries have had days on which people honored their dead parents. The Romans celebrated Parentalia from February 13 to February 22 by decorating family graves and having a family feast. Asian countries and African societies have for many centuries set aside a day or more each year in honor of their ancestors. Celebrations have often been family reunions at which stories and histories of the dead would be told. In this way children could learn of their families and their past.

20 West Virginia — Admission Day

When can a riddle become a father?
When the answer becomes apparent.

22 Summer Solstice The Summer Solstice (a word from the Latin meaning "sun stands still") occurs when the sun appears to be at its highest point in the sky. It is the longest day and the shortest night of the year. At that time, usually about June 22 in the Northern Hemisphere, the sun is directly overhead at noon at the Tropic of Cancer. It seems to stay in the same position in the sky—to stand still—for several days. The solstice marks the beginning of summer in the present calendar, but is called Midsummer Day because it was celebrated long before there were calendars. Since ancient days there have been fire ceremonies throughout Europe on Midsummer Eve and Midsummer Day. The ceremonies honored the sun, applauded its long stay in the sky, and tried to scare the evil spirits who might try to make trouble. (Scaring evil spirits was an important part of most old holidays.) Bonfires were lit—often in rings around a town or meeting place — and torches and lanterns were carried in parades. In many countries flowers and grains were thrown into the flames to ask the sun to shine on the crops. Lovers jumped over the flames holding hands to bring themselves good luck and a long life together. Cattle and sheep were led close to the fire to breathe in the "lucky" smoke. Ashes from the fires were thrown on the fields and placed in barns and houses to bring good luck and long life. (See December 22.)

If you pick a rose on Midsummer Day and put it away without looking at it again, it will still be fresh on Christmas Day.
Old English superstition

24 St. John the Baptist's Day When Christianity reached Europe, a Christian holiday celebrating the birth of St. John the Baptist was combined with the midsummer festivities. Jesus had called John his "burning light." St. John's Day is celebrated in much of Europe, South America, and Canada with the traditional fires. (See November 19.)

The ghosts of dogs walk on St. John's Eve, but they can only be seen by dogs.
Old English superstition

JULY

1 Dominion Day — Canada On July 1, 1867, Upper and Lower Canada and some of the Maritime Provinces agreed to form the Dominion of Canada. The anniversary of the event was declared a national holiday which is celebrated with parades and speeches.

3 Dog Days The period from July 3 to August 11 — the hottest days of the year in the Northern Hemisphere — is called the Dog Days. Since the earliest years Dog Days have been thought to be evil and unhealthy — a time when rain seldom falls, the sea boils, flies increase, dogs and people go mad, and snakes go blind and bite at anything that disturbs them. Despite the heat, an old English and American superstition, still believed by many, says that it is unhealthy to swim during the Dog Days. In ancient times Sirius, the Dog Star, rose at about sunrise each day during the hot period, and this is how the Dog Days got their name. Sirius was thought to cause the hot, humid weather and a brown dog was sacrificed each year to calm the anger of the star.

4 Independence Day Independence Day, or the Fourth of July, celebrates the signing of the Declaration of Independence at Philadelphia in 1776. In fact, the only people who signed the document on July 4 were John Hancock (see January 23) and Charles Thomson, the president and secretary of the Continental Congress. The official signing of the Declaration of Independence by fifty persons took place on August 2, 1776. Five more men signed later, one a whole year later. But the first signing, on July 4, 1776, made it clear to Americans, to England, and to the rest of the world that the colonies would fight Britain for their independence. Independence Day was first celebrated in 1777, while the war was being fought and independence was still not a certainty. The celebration, held in Philadelphia, was one of speeches, bell ringing, and bonfires and fireworks — very much like modern celebrations on the Fourth of July. What was important about the original Fourth of July was not the event — the signing of the Declaration of Independence — but the idea behind that event: liberty and justice for all.

Thomas Jefferson and John Adams both died on July 4, 1826. The day was the fiftieth anniversary of the Declaration of Independence, which they had both signed. A few years later, in 1831, another former president, James Monroe, died on July 4.

Can you name the capital of all the states in just thirty seconds?
Washington, D.C.

Which countries, besides the U.S.A., have a fourth of July?
All of them—also a third and a fifth.

What does the United States produce that no other country can?
U.S. citizens.

6 Beatrix Potter's Birthday Beatrix Potter, born in London, England, on July 6 1866, was the author and illustrator of the Peter Rabbit stories. At first she had to publish her stories at her own expense, since no publisher thought that they were good enough to sell more than a few copies.

Can you spell rabbit without using the letter R?
BUNNY.

7 Star Festival — Japan At the beginning of the Star Festival — called Tanabata in Japanese — bamboo branches are placed upright in the ground. Children write poems, print them on strips of colored paper or cloth, and tie them to the bamboo branches—all in honor of the stars.

What letter can move a star?
The letter T can make a star start.

Most of the stars that can be seen from earth with an unaided eye are brighter than the sun.

10 Wyoming—Admission Day

14 Bastille Day — France In 1789 the Bastille, a state prison in Paris, was captured and partly destroyed by members of the French Revolution. The capture of the Bastille encouraged the revolutionary party to carry on its fight for freedom from the rule of the king and his nobles. After the revolution was won, when the monarchy was overthrown and the people of France were in control of the government, Bastille Day became the major political holiday of the country. The holiday is also celebrated in other countries to mark the importance of independence and freedom.

15 St. Swithin's Day St. Swithin was a bishop in England in the 800s. When he was dying, he asked to be buried outside the church, so that the "sweet rain of heaven might fall on my grave." This was done, but when the bishop was made a saint, the monks decided to move his body inside the church. On the fifteenth of July, when they went to move the body, heavy rains made the work impossible. The rain continued for forty days until the monks gave up their plan. An English superstition says that if it rains on St. Swithin's Day, it will rain for forty days; and if the sun shines on St. Swithin's Day, it will remain fair for forty days.

Clement Clarke Moore's Birthday Moore wrote the poem "A Visit from Saint Nicholas," better known by its first verse, "'Twas the night before Christmas." The poem was first published, without Moore's permission, in a Troy, New York, newspaper, on December 23, 1823.

20 Moon Day Moon Day marks the anniversary of the first human landing on the moon at 4:17 P.M., eastern daylight time, July 20, 1969. The landing was made from the United States' Apollo 11 command module *Columbia* piloted by Michael Collins. Collins remained aboard the *Columbia* while astronauts Neil Armstrong and Edwin "Buzz" Aldrin, Jr., landed on the moon in the lunar module *Eagle*. The landing lasted for twenty-one hours, thirty-six minutes, and twenty seconds, but Armstrong and Aldrin were outside of the lunar module and walked on the moon for about two hours and fifteen minutes. Armstrong was the first to step onto the surface of the moon.

The moon is an average distance of 239,000 miles from earth.

When is it impossible to land on the moon?
When it is full.

25 Puerto Rico—Constitution Day
26 New York—Ratification Day
29 Norway—Olsok Eve Bonfires and historical plays celebrate St. Olaf, the Viking king of Norway, who was killed in battle on July 29, 1030.

AUGUST

1 National Clown Week To honor clowns, and to encourage the wonderful and wacky art of clowning, the clowns of America celebrate the first week of August each year as National Clown Week.

August was named for the Roman emperor Augustus Caesar.

Fewer holidays, anniversaries, memorial days, and special events are celebrated in August than in any other month.

3 Columbus' Sailing Anniversary Just before sunrise on Friday, August 3, 1492, Christopher Columbus set sail from Palos, Spain, in search of a new route to the Orient. The tall red-haired Italian commanded three small ships—the *Nina*, the *Pinta*, and the *Santa Maria*—with a combined crew of ninety sailors. More than two months later, land was sighted. (See October 12.) The land was not China—although Columbus always believed that it was—but one of the smaller islands of the Bahamas miles south of the American Continent. Columbus opened the way for the exploration and settlement of the New World, but he was not rewarded by having the continent named after him. That honor was reserved for Amerigo Vespucci, who first made clear that the land was *new* and not part of Asia.

Columbus' sailors brought the habit of tobacco smoking from the New World back to Spain. One of the men, Rodrigo de Jerez, was accused by his wife to the church as being possessed by the devil because he swallowed fire and blew out smoke.

Many of the men who sailed with Columbus were criminals who were promised their freedom if they would take the terrible journey into the unknown.

In 1492 ships often had nicknames as well as true names. The Santa Maria is the only one of Columbus' ships that we call by her true name; her nickname was La Gallega, "the Galician," because she was built in Galicia. The Nina's real name was Santa Clara; her nickname came from her owners, the Nino family. No one knows the Pinta's real name; her nickname probably came from the name of her owner.

How do we know that Christopher Columbus was thrifty?
He traveled 30,000 miles on a galleon.

6 Hiroshima Day Memorial services are held in Japan and many other places for the victims of the first atomic bombing at Hiroshima, Japan, by the United States, on August 6, 1945.

10 Missouri—Admission Day
11 Victory Day—Rhode Island
14 Liberty Hill Day—Massachusetts
17 Hawaii—Admission Day

19 National Aviation Day By presidential proclamation (see page 32) National Aviation Day has been observed each August 19 since 1939. The holiday is celebrated on the birthday of aviation pioneer Orville Wright. Orville Wright and his brother, Wilbur, made aviation history at Kitty Hawk, North Carolina, with the first controlled flight in a power-driven airplane. Their first flight took only twelve seconds, and the distance flown was shorter than the length of the wings of a modern jumbo jet.

Two wrongs never make a right, but what did two rights make?
The first airplane.
Who invented the first flightless airplane?
The Wrong brothers.
What would you get if you crossed an SST and a kangaroo?
A fast airplane that made short hops.

26 Women's Equality Day On August 26, 1920, the Nineteenth Amendment, which made it possible for women to vote, was accepted as part of the Constitution of the United States. (See February 15.)

Which bus crossed the ocean?
Columbus.

How do we know that
Christopher Columbus was thrifty?
He traveled 30,000 miles
on a galleon.

What is the difference
between the lid of a dish
and Christopher Columbus?
One is a dish cover
and the other a discoverer.

Columbus discovered America,
but who was the first person
to circle the earth?
The man in the moon.

SEPTEMBER

★ **Labor Day** In the United States and Canada, the laborer is honored on the first Monday in September. The holiday was first celebrated in the United States in 1882 and became a federal holiday in 1894. In most countries, however, and in many places in the United States and Canada, the laborer is honored on May Day instead (see May 1). Often, Labor Day is not really celebrated — it just marks the end of summer vacations and the beginning of the new school year.

4 Los Angeles, California's Birthday The city of Los Angeles was founded on September 4, 1781. Its full name is *El Pueblo de Nuestra Señora La Reina de Los Angeles de Porciuncula.*

5 Be Late for Something Day The Procrastinators' Club of America (see March: National Procrastination Week) celebrates Be Late for Something Day to help people relax from the strain of always being on time. Some people celebrate Be Late for Something Day a day or two late.

9 California — Admission Day

★ **Grandparents' Day** The first Sunday after Labor Day honors grandparents, by presidential proclamation (see page 32).

12 Charles Dudley Warner's Birthday Warner was the American newspaperman who originally wrote in an editorial in 1897, "Everybody talks about the weather, but nobody does anything about it."

◗ **Rosh Hashanah** The Hebrew words *Rosh Hashanah* mean "the head of the year," the name for the Jewish New Year. Traditionally it is said that the world was created on Rosh Hashanah over 5700 years ago, and in some Hebrew schools the children sing "Happy Birthday World." Rosh Hashanah is celebrated on the first two days of the Hebrew month of Tishri — usually in September or October (see March: The Hebrew Year). The holiday begins the High Holy Days, a sacred time of the year when Jews pray, remember their sins of the past year, repent those sins, and vow to do better. During this time, Jews believe, God judges people and writes the judgment in the Book of Life. The New Year's greeting in Hebrew is "Leshanah tovah tikatevu" — "May you be inscribed in the Book of Life for a good year."

Many of the Jewish New Year customs have to do with food and may have started before Judaism with the harvest festivals of earlier religions. Honey cakes and pieces of apple dipped in honey are eaten to symbolize a sweet year to come. The Jewish bread, *challah,* is baked in a round loaf, to symbolize the round, whole year. And a special dish called *tsimmes* is made of carrots. Because the Hebrew word for carrot means to "increase," the food is eaten in hopes of increased goodness in the new year.

◗ **Yom Kippur** The Jewish High Holy Days end with Yom Kippur. On this day, Jews believe, God judges them and writes his final decision in the Book of Life. Long ago, Jews thought that the sins of people could be transferred to animals. Yom Kippur was the day on which special services were held to give people's sins to animals — usually goats called "scapegoats." Two or more goats were chosen to carry the sins of a community. One of the goats was killed in the temple, the other was driven into the desert — each taking sins with him. By 70 C.E., however, the Jews realized that each person must accept responsibility for his or her own errors. In modern times the entire day is spent at the synagogue. Anyone over thirteen years of age must fast all day, and anyone younger may fast if he or she chooses. The rabbi wears white robes to symbolize the purity of the days to come, and the synagogue is decorated with white flowers. The story of Jonah and the whale is read because in it God explains the importance of forgiving people who are sorry for their sins and errors.

◑ Sukkoth A few days after the end of the Jewish High Holy Days comes the Jewish harvest festival of Sukkoth. It is an eight-day holiday of thanksgiving for all growing plants, a festival that most likely has roots in pre-Jewish harvest festivals.

◑ Simchat Torah On the day after Sukkoth ends, Jewish people celebrate the joyous festival of Simchat Torah, which means "Rejoicing in the Torah." Parts of the Torah, the books of the Law, are read aloud in the synagogue each day. Simchat Torah is the day on which the reading is ended and begun anew — showing that the Torah has no beginning and no end but goes on forever. The congregation marches seven times around the synagogue, led by the rabbi and the elders carrying Torahs. Children wave flags, sing songs, and dance around the procession. The youngest ride on the shoulders of the men. Candy is eaten so that everyone remembers the sweetness of the Torah.

23 Autumnal Equinox The date on which the sun crosses the celestial equator from north to south is the Autumnal Equinox. It marks the beginning of fall in the Northern Hemisphere. On that date, usually September 23, day and night are of equal length; then the days start to get shorter. (See March 21.)

Birthdays!

Birthdays, or days on which names are given, are celebrated in many countries. A birthday cake and candles as part of the festivities go back many hundreds, even thousands, of years. Fire has always been important because it gave protection against man and beasts. And evil spirits, as well as living animals, were believed to be afraid of the flames. Once the need for a real fire was gone, candles were used as a symbol of protection and are still lit on important occasions — including birthdays. Originally the birthday candles were lit to frighten away the evil spirits who were said to come to bring bad luck when people gathered in happiness. A wish, made while blowing the candles out, was thought to be likely to come true because evil spirits would be distracted by the change in light.

Writing from holy books of any religion has often been used as a protection against evil and illness. Sometimes special charms asking for long life and other good things were written on food and the food eaten. The person who ate the food was supposed to gain the power of the charm. The practice of writing "Happy Birthday" or "Good Wishes" on cakes most likely came from this belief.

26 Johnny Appleseed's Birthday John Chapman was known to settlers of Pennsylvania, Indiana, and Ohio in the early 1800s as Johnny Appleseed. He walked through the frontier states — where there were no fruit trees — clearing places in the fields and forests and planting appleseeds. Later he returned to care for the young trees and to help the farmers plant more. Many people laughed at Chapman's odd dress and speech, but the laughter was friendly and Johnny Appleseed and his trees were always welcomed.

To eat an apple without rubbing it first is to challenge the devil.
Old English superstition

An old superstition says that you can find out your fate in love by counting the seeds of an apple, saying:

One, I love,
Two, I love,
Three, I love, I say,
Four, I love with all my heart,
And five, I cast away.

Six, he loves,
Seven, she loves,
Eight, they both love.
Nine, he comes,
Ten, he tarries,
Eleven, he courts,
Twelve, he marries.
Thirteen wishes,
Fourteen kisses,
All the rest, little witches.

To choose between two lovers, take two apple seeds, name one for each lover, spit on the seeds, and stick them on your forehead. The seed that stays on the longest shows who is the right lover for you.

★Good Neighbor Day The fourth Sunday in September, by presidential proclamation (see page 32) is National Good Neighbor Day. It is a day to visit the sick and help the elderly, the lonely, the handicapped, and the newcomers to the neighborhood. In some towns and cities, schoolchildren or whole classes help to clean up the neighborhood, paint houses, rake lawns, or bake cookies for those who cannot do such work themselves. Many people find that by making a neighbor happy they make themselves happy.

OCTOBER

★ Child Health Day/Universal Children's Day By presidential proclamation (see page 32), the first Monday in October is Child Health Day. Meant to encourage good health care for children, the holiday was first celebrated in the United States on May 1, 1928. The date of the observance was changed by an act of Congress in 1959 so that it would fall on the day named by the United Nations as Universal Children's Day.

9 Leif Ericson Day In the year 999 the Norse explorer Leif Ericson set sail across the uncharted northern seas. Leif, called the Lucky, started his journey in a Viking serpent ship when he was only twenty years old. A year later he became the first European to land in North America — first in central Labrador and later in southern Labrador or Newfoundland. The site of his third landing is uncertain; it may have been Cape Cod, Martha's Vineyard, or Long Island, New York. He named the place where he landed the third time "Vinland the Good." Leif and his men spent the winter in the New World before going home to Norway. Other Vikings returned to Vinland to start a colony. Traces of that or another settlement have been found in Newfoundland — an iron smelter, cooking pots, and a spinning tool. Although there were recorded histories of Ericson's journey and of the short-lived settlements, the maps were unclear and the news did not spread throughout Europe. Almost 500 years later, when Columbus set sail from Spain, the Viking discoveries were unknown or had been forgotten in southern Europe.

12 Traditional Columbus Day The lookout on the smallest of Columbus's ships, the *Pinta,* first saw land at two in the morning on October 12, 1492. The sighting came two days after a near mutiny during which Columbus promised his sailors he would turn back if land were not found within three days. The land sighted was an island in the Bahamas which Columbus named San Salvador, or "Holy Savior." The island is now known as Watlings Island. (See August 3.)

★ Columbus Day By presidential proclamation (see page 32) the second Monday in October is observed as Columbus Day. The holiday is now celebrated on this day — with parades and parties — in most states. Columbus Day was first celebrated in the United States in 1792, on the three-hundredth anniversary of Columbus's landing. Soon after, the government of the new United States named the area where its capital would be the District of Columbia in honor of Columbus.

Early Portuguese explorers carried convicts on their first trips to South America. In areas where the inhabitants were unknown, the convicts were thrown overboard to find out if the natives were cannibals. Luckily none were.

★ Discoverers' Day — Hawaii In Hawaii, the second Monday in October honors not only Columbus but all discoverers, including the Polynesian navigators who explored the Pacific Ocean islands.

16 Noah Webster's Birthday Webster compiled the earliest American dictionary in the English language.

★ Hurricane Thanksgiving Day — Virgin Islands In the Virgin Islands, where the threat of hurricanes is great during the summer and early fall months, the third Monday in October is a legal holiday celebrating the end of hurricane season.

23 Swallows depart from San Juan Capistrano It is said — and often happens — that the swallows of San Juan Capistrano Mission in California arrive each May 19 and depart for the winter each year on October 23. The departure date is the anniversary of the death of St. John — San Juan — of Capistrano after whom the mission is named.

★**National Popcorn Week** The last week in October honors popcorn as a healthy, economical, and natural food. Popcorn is a native American food — it was given to the first colonists in Plymouth, Massachusetts, by the American Indians.

31 Nevada — Admission Day

Halloween, or All Hallows' Eve Halloween combines the autumn festival of the Druids, the customs of one of the great witches' sabbaths of the old religion which existed in Europe before Christianity, and Christian customs and beliefs. The origins of the holiday are very old and reach back even beyond farming societies to hunting societies. The festival once marked the beginning of the winter animal breeding season. The earliest celebrations were held in the open fields, the evening before the holiday. Torches, lanterns, and candles lit the way to the meeting place. Large fall turnips, potatoes, and other solid vegetables were hollowed out and used as holders to help carry the candles without dripping hot wax. Slits or faces were cut in the vegetables to let more light shine through. Apples — still an important part of Halloween celebrations — were carried to eat, as were small packages of food. Great fires were lit, and people often danced around their light. Animals were sometimes sacrificed in hopes of increased births in the season to come.

What do you call a misspelled word on a tombstone?
A grave mistake.

In England the ancient Britons celebrated their Druid New Year on November 1, so that the last night of October was New Year's Eve. The fires were meant to frighten off the spirits believed to gather to discuss who was to die in the year to come. People dressed as ghosts to fool the spirits of the dead into thinking that only a few living people were at the celebration. Some people believed that on New Year's Eve the souls of people who had sinned passed into animals. Animals and even humans were sacrificed to keep the spirits too busy with the souls of the dead to bother with those of the living. When the Romans invaded England and other parts of Europe, they stopped the sacrifices, but many of the other customs continued. The celebration was adopted by the Christians in the 700s as All Hallows' Eve and All Hallows' Day — a time to honor all the saints of the Church who were not honored by an individual day. The name of the holiday we now celebrate comes from the Christian holiday, but most of the customs and superstitions about Halloween are more pagan than Christian.

On Halloween all the souls in hell are released for forty-eight hours.

If you stand at a crossroad at midnight on Halloween and listen to the wind, you will hear the voices of the dead talking about all the important things that will happen to you during the coming year.
English superstition

Apples are part of many Halloween superstitions and customs. One, which is followed in some form in many parts of the world, comes from very old religious practices. It is said that if you peel an apple in a single strip on Halloween and throw the skin over your left shoulder, you will read the initials of your true love in the twists of the skin. The superstition may be based on the old Druid, Greek, and Roman customs of telling the future from the twisted entrails of sacrificed animals.

How does a witch know when it is midnight on Halloween?
She looks at her witch watch.

In places near the sea, it is often believed that on Halloween all those who have died by drowning come up to ride over the waves on "white horses."

To keep yourself safe from witches on Halloween, carry a piece of iron in your pocket. Witches cannot stand the presence of iron.

Standard time begins at 2:00 A.M. on the last Sunday in October.

The more there is of it, the less
you can see. What is it?
Darkness.

If you see a ghost
chasing twelve trick-or-treaters
down the block, what time is it?
One after twelve.

NOVEMBER

1 All Saints' Day The Christian church honors the saints not honored on any other day on All Saints' Day — a feast day known in medieval times as Hallowmas or All Hallows' Day. The idea of having a holiday for all the unknown saints, or gods, so that none would feel angry or left out, did not start with Christianity. The Greeks, for example, had twelve major gods and each one had his or her own holiday. There were also dozens of minor Greek gods who had special days of celebration. The Greeks were afraid, however, that they might have missed a god, who would be angry and would bring bad luck to the community. To avoid this, once a year the Greeks celebrated the Feast of the Unknown Gods.

In ancient and modern times, certain stones have been connected with each month as "lucky" stones or birthstones. The stone associated with November is the topaz and is supposed to have the special quality of aiding in friendships and of helping to guard the wearer against calamity. The stones for the other months are January—garnet, February—amethyst, March—aquamarine, April—diamond, May—emerald, June—pearl, July—ruby, August—peridot, September—sapphire, October—opal, December—turquoise.

2 North Dakota — Admission Day
South Dakota — Admission Day

5 Guy Fawkes Day — United Kingdom On November 5, 1605, Guy Fawkes, as part of a religious conflict in England, tried to blow up the House of Parliament in London. But, just as the meetings were being opened by King James I, thirty-six barrels of explosives — ready to be set afire — were found in the basement of the House of Lords. Guy Fawkes Day is remembered in the United Kingdom with fireworks, bonfires, and the hanging and burning of straw dummies of the plotters. Because of the nearness of the two holidays, many of the customs of Halloween are used on Guy Fawkes Day. Children dress in funny costumes, parade around, and often beg for pennies or food. The night before Guy Fawkes Day is celebrated in some parts of England as Mischief Night.

★**Election Day** In the United States, the first Tuesday after the first Monday in November is Election Day. Everywhere in the country the day is set aside for the election of officials in national, state, county, and city governments. Everybody over age eighteen who has committed no serious crime, is mentally sound, has lived in the community for a certain length of time, and has registered in the community may vote in the elections. In the United States since the 1860s most voting has been done by secret ballot, so that only the voter knows what he or she has marked on the ballot or vote. Voting in secret helps protect the voter from the opinions and pressures of others. Citizens of the United States don't *have* to vote, but voting is one of the major ways in which a citizen can participate in his or her self-government.

11 Armistice Day, Veterans Day, Remembrance Day
World War I ended at the eleventh hour of the eleventh day of the eleventh month of 1918. Many countries observe that day each year as a public holiday of prayer and remembrance. In some countries there is a moment of silence at exactly 11:00 A.M. By presidential proclamation (see page 32) the federal government now celebrates November 11 each year as Veterans Day. In 1970 an attempt was made to change the date of Veterans Day to the fourth Monday in October; but separating Veterans Day from the date of the ending of World War I proved unpopular, and the holiday was moved back to the traditional date of November 11 in 1978. In Canada, November 11 is a public holiday called Remembrance Day.

✖ **St. Martin's Day** In much of Europe November 11 is the feast of St. Martin, or Martinmas. The feast is part of an old harvest festival that is celebrated by eating roast goose and drinking the sweet new wine. In Germany, Switzerland, the Netherlands, and parts of Scandinavia, the children make jack-o'-lanterns out of turnips and parade with them through the streets.

If Saint Martin's Day is cold, the winter will be short and mild.
Old English and southern American superstition

✖ **Children's Book Week** Once books for children did nothing but teach lessons. Every book had a moral. No child's book was written simply to amuse the child or to be read just for pleasure. Today the third full week of November, starting on Monday, is celebrated in schools, libraries, and communities as National Children's Book Week. Special programs and displays emphasize the importance of reading—to learn, to grow, to amuse, to enjoy. Book weeks have been celebrated since 1912 and have been sponsored by the Children's Book Council since 1945.

Can you make a long book from the nine letters OLAKGOONB?
A LONG BOOK.
What color is a book when you've finished reading it?
Red.

If you drop a schoolbook, you must kiss it as you pick it up or you will forget everything you have read in it.
European superstition

What is an author's business like?
All write.
Why is a poor writer like a hero?
Because he writes wrong.

16 Oklahoma — Admission Day

19 Puerto Rico — Discovery Day On November 19, 1493, on his second voyage to the New World, Columbus landed on an island to get clean water. The Indians living on the island told him that its name was Borinquén, but, as was the custom of European explorers, Columbus renamed the island. The new name was San Juan Bautista, for St. John the Baptist (see June 24). One of the men who sailed with Columbus, Ponce de León, returned to the island in 1508 and established a waterside colony, which he named Porto Rico, or "Rich Port." A mapmaker made a mistake and recorded the city as San Juan and the island as Puerto Rico, and we continue to use these names today.

21 North Carolina — Ratification Day

✖ **Thanksgiving Day** By presidential proclamation (see page 32) the fourth Thursday in November is Thanksgiving Day. Every state observes this day as a legal public holiday. Thanksgiving is the first United States holiday ever celebrated by presidential proclamation. George Washington proclaimed November 26, 1789, as Thanksgiving Day after Congress asked him to name a day of public thanksgiving and prayer for the time of prosperity, freedom, and hope after the long war. Thanksgiving days had been celebrated by the

colonists since the first days of the settlements. Early Virginia colonists landed in December 1619. They celebrated a day of thanksgiving for their safe arrival and proclaimed that their arrival day, December 4, should be celebrated each year. The Pilgrims who landed in Plymouth, Massachusetts, in November 1620 celebrated a thanksgiving day after the first harvest to give thanks for having lived through the dangers of the past year. The last Thursday in November was chosen as the national day of thanksgiving by President Lincoln in 1863. In 1939 President Franklin D. Roosevelt tried to change the holiday to the third Thursday in November because of the short time between the last Thursday and Christmas. But the outcry from the traditionalists was too loud; the holiday was returned to the fourth Thursday in November in 1941. Now Thanksgiving is most often celebrated as a family, rather than a public, holiday. Although there are religious services in some communities, most people celebrate Thanksgiving by gathering together as a family and eating too much turkey, stuffing, cranberry sauce, sweet potatoes, green beans, pumpkin pie, and mince pie. Many recover from the meal by taking naps or watching the football game — a new national tradition.

What did the pumpkin pie say to the turkey?
I can beat the stuffing out of you.

Why can't you have guests for Thanksgiving dinner?
You can, but turkey is more traditional.

Why didn't the turkey eat any supper?
Because she was stuffed.

What happened to the boy who talked with food in his mouth?
He said a mouthful.

The Pilgrims probably didn't eat turkey at the first Thanksgiving dinner they shared with the Indians. Turkey wasn't a special food then; it was an everyday item. Thanksgiving dinner was probably deer—brought by the Indians—and lobsters and clams gathered by the settlers. There would also have been onions and corn pudding.

29 Louisa May Alcott's Birthday

Why did the turkey cross the road? So no one would think he was chicken.

DECEMBER

6 St. Nicholas's Day — Europe St. Nicholas, a bishop in the city of Myra in Asia Minor in the fourth century, is the patron saint of children and sailors. No one is too sure what the original St. Nicholas was like, but there are many legends about him — perhaps some are even true. In one legend, St. Nicholas was said to bring back to life three boys who had been chopped up and pickled in salt by a butcher. In another he saved three girls from being sold into slavery by giving their poor father three golden balls. The three balls later became the symbol of pawnbrokers. St. Nicholas's Day is celebrated in many European countries as the Christmas season gift-giving holiday. There are often parades with St. Nicholas, dressed differently in different countries, leading the way. (See December 25.)

10 Human Rights Day The United Nations has asked all member states to observe December 10 each year as Human Rights Day. It is a day set aside to consider, and help strengthen, the basic freedoms to which all the people of the world are entitled. By presidential proclamation (see page 32) the United States observes Human Rights Day each December 10.

12 Pennsylvania — Ratification Day

13 St. Lucia's Day — Sweden Lucia was a young girl who lived in Sicily about 300 A.D. She was blinded and then executed on December 13 by the Romans because she would not give up her belief in the Christian religion. The day on which St. Lucia was killed was, according to the old style calendar, the Winter Solstice (see December 22). The Winter Solstice is the shortest day of the year, after which it begins to stay light a little longer each day. Because Lucia was killed on the solstice, and because her name means "light," her day was adopted as an important holiday by the Vikings — people from the far north who first invaded Sicily and then became Christian. In the Scandinavian countries where the Vikings lived, Winter Solstice festivals had long been celebrated to greet the lengthening days and the return of light (see December 22). St. Lucia's Day continued these customs.

Now, in Sweden, the eldest daughter in each home dresses as St. Lucia, in a white gown with a crown of green leaves and candles. She and her sisters, also dressed in white and carrying candles, take special "Lucia buns" from house to house.

14 Alabama — Admission Day

◗Chanukah In 165 B.C.E. the Jews of Israel had fallen under the control of the Greeks. Jews were not allowed to rule themselves or to practice their religion; the temple in Jerusalem had even been made unclean. A group of Jews led by the Maccabee brothers, fought to deliver their people from the Greeks. When the Maccabees succeeded, the first thing they did was rededicate the temple. Part of the ceremony included relighting the "Eternal Light," which was never supposed to go out. Only enough pure oil was found in the temple, however, to burn for one day. For unexplained reasons the oil continued to burn for eight days — until messengers arrived with new oil. Today Chanukah is celebrated for eight days, starting on the twenty-fifth of the Hebrew month of Kislev (see March: The Hebrew Year). Gifts are given on each day of the holiday — at least a small present, often money — as the candles are lit in memory of the light that burned eight days. Chanukah is often called the Festival of Lights. There are Chanukah parties with special songs, dances, games, and foods. One special treat is potato *latkes,* or pancakes, made with pure vegetable oil to symbolize the oil found in the temple.

15 Halcyon Days The seven-day period before and after the Winter Solstice was thought by ancient peoples to be a time of special quiet in the world of nature. A huge bird was said to come down from the skies to calm the wind and the waves, and animals and birds stayed quietly in their dens and nests.

16 Anniversary of the Boston Tea Party

22 Winter Solstice The Winter Solstice (a word from the Latin meaning "sun stands still") occurs when the sun appears to be at its lowest point in the sky. It is the shortest day and longest night of the year. At that time, usually about December 22 in the Northern Hemisphere, the sun is directly overhead at noon in the Tropic of Capricorn. It seems to stay in the same position in the sky — to stand still — for several days. The solstice marks the beginning of winter. The Winter Solstice festivals which were held in most of the northern world, honored the sun and drove away the winter demons with bonfires and flaming candles and logs (see December 13). Houses were decorated with holly, a tree honored by the ancient Druid priests because it remained green all year and even bore fruit — red berries — in the winter. The Druids took the holly as a sign that life would go on all year. Mistletoe was honored by the Druids as a sign of friendship and peace, since mistletoe grew on and took nourishment from oak trees without harming them. In the north European countries it was believed that enemies who stood together under mistletoe would become friends. (See June 22.)

25 Christmas Day When Christianity moved north and across Europe, the Winter Solstice festival of the pagans became an important winter festival for the Christians. At first the holiday did not celebrate the birth of Jesus, but the "light" of the gospel. No one knows exactly when Jesus was born. For the first four centuries of Christianity, his birth was celebrated on days which had special meaning for the pagans: March 25 — the Vernal Equinox, November 17 — a traditional harvest festival in southern Europe, December 25 — the time of the Winter Solstice, January 6 — the time of the water puri-

Bees hum the One-Hundredth Psalm on Christmas Eve.

fication festival in Egypt. A meeting of the Christian bishops in 440 A.D. decided to celebrate the birth of Jesus each year at the time of the Winter Solstice, the most important pagan festival. In that way, people could become Christian without having to give up their favorite holiday. Most of the customs of the Winter Solstice celebration were carried over into the Christian celebration — the bonfires, the candles, the burning of large logs, and the use of holly, mistletoe, and other evergreens for decoration (see December 22). In countries where gifts are not given on St. Nicholas's Day (see December 6), they are usually given on either Christmas Eve or Christmas Day. No matter when gifts are given, St. Nicholas is usually part of the celebration. The Dutch, who founded the city that is now New York, first brought St. Nicholas to the New World. The English colonists shortened his Dutch name — *Sint Nikolaas* or *Sinter Klaas* — to Santa Claus and moved his feast day to the English gift-giving holiday of Christmas. Today, the Winter Solstice customs of the ancient pagans, the legends and characteristics of St. Nicholas, and the traditions of the Christian celebration of the birth of Jesus all combine to make a winter holiday of Christmas — a joyous joining of folkways and religion.

The Pilgrim fathers did not allow the early colonists in Massachusetts to celebrate Christmas. They thought that the traditional celebrations were too worldly and full of fun and not respectful enough.

31 New Year's Eve Pagan and non-Christian holidays generally start at sundown the day before the holiday, since according to the lunar calendar a day starts at sundown. When the use of the new solar calendar became widespread (see January 1), the custom of starting the holidays in the evening remained part of the celebrations. (See February: Lunar New Year, April 1, October 31.)

Windows should be opened for a few minutes just before midnight on New Year's Eve to let the bad luck out and the good luck in. General superstition

What is the first thing you do on Christmas morning?
You wake up.

When can you kick about a gift?
When it's a soccer ball.

What is a beatnik?
Santa Claus the day after Christmas.

Why did one of Santa's eight elves wake up late every morning?
The alarm was set for seven.

Proclaimed by the President...

In the United States, all federal public holidays, and all special days, weeks, and months of celebration or commemoration are proclaimed by the president. The president can proclaim the holiday directly, but frequently the day is passed through Congress to the president for approval and proclamation.

The procedure for passage through the Congress starts with acceptance by a member of the House of Representatives. A citizen or group of citizens who wish to have a proclamation for a special day issued must first convince their representative that the special day would benefit the nation. Once convinced, the representative writes the request for a special day as a resolution to be introduced into the House of Representatives.

Once the resolution is introduced into the House, it must get the backing—co-sponsorship—of the majority of the House, at least 218 co-sponsors. When the resolution has at least 218 co-sponsors, it goes to a subcommittee and then to the entire Post Office and Civil Service Committee of the House of Representatives. This committee has the responsibility of approving or disapproving resolutions for special days.

The Post Office Committee considers special days three times a year—February, June, and October. Although it approves a number of different days, the committee has a policy of not considering any proposal
1 about a product, a commercial enterprise, or a fraternal, political, or sectarian organization,
2 about a state or other political unit or school or institution of higher learning,
3 about a living person,
4 for a recurring annual event.

If the Post Office Committee approves it, the resolution is voted on by the House and should receive a majority of House votes because it already has 218 co-sponsors. Once the resolution passes the House, it goes to the Senate. If the resolution passes the Senate—which usually does pass a resolution accepted by the House—it goes to the president. The president usually accepts the resolution and has it written up as a presidential proclamation and printed in the Federal Register.

Each year over 500 resolutions are brought to the House by a representative. Fewer than ten are passed and become the subject of presidential proclamations. Many people are disappointed, of course, but if all 500 were accepted each year, every day would have at least one holiday.

Special days of celebration or commemoration and holidays can also be proclaimed directly by the president. In general, the president follows the policies of the Post Office Committee of the House of Representatives. Unlike the House committee, however, the president can, and does, consider days which will recur—happen year after year—as well as one-time only holidays. All holidays proclaimed directly through the president or through the Congress must have national appeal and significance. So if you have a day you want proclaimed by the president, make sure before you talk to your representative that the day will be of interest and concern to the entire nation, not just to your community.